LiCe are LoUsY!

Library of Congress Cataloging-in-Publication Data
Tsubakiyama, Margaret.
Lice are lousy! : all about headlice / by Margaret Tsubakiyama.
p. cm.
Summary: A brief history of head lice, with information about how
infestations start, the life cycle of the louse, and what can be done
to get rid of lice.
ISBN 0-7613-1316-8 (lib. bdg.)
1. Pediculosis—Juvenile literature. [1. Pediculosis. 2. Lice.] I. Title.
RL764.P4T75   1999
616.5'7—dc21   98-26730   CIP   AC

Published by The Millbrook Press, Inc.
2 Old New Milford Road
Brookfield, CT 06804

Lice are Lousy!

All About Headlice

Margaret Tsubakiyama

Illustrations by
Anne Canevari Green

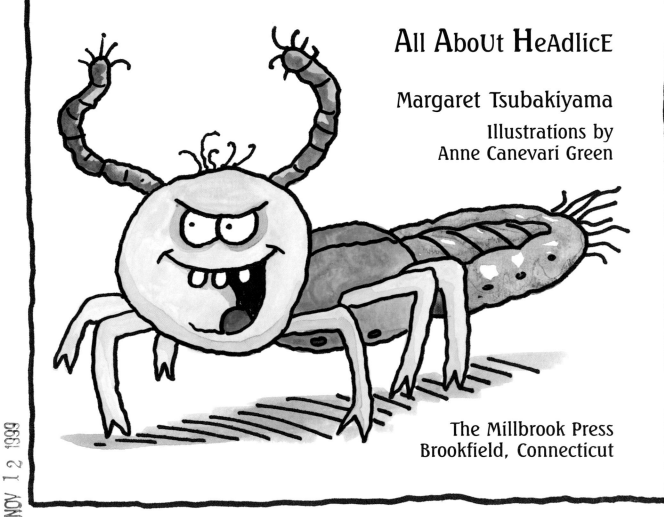

The Millbrook Press
Brookfield, Connecticut

Do you scratch your head when you think? Do you scratch your head when you study? Do you scratch your head when you sleep, run, walk, play soccer, watch TV, or eat potato chips? If so, then you may have pediculosis (peh-dik-u-LO-sis)—headlice.

If you're itching, you're not alone. Lice have been making people itch for a very long time. Scientists have even found mummified lice in ancient tombs.

In the Middle Ages, everybody had lice—young people, old people, rich people, poor people. Nobody was embarrassed about it. It was totally normal to invite your best friend over to help pick off your lice.

When George Washington lived, lots of people still had lice. So did George. When he was thirteen years old, he wrote a book about manners.

In his book he says that it is not polite to kill your own fleas or lice when other people are watching. However, if you see a louse on another person, it is polite to brush it away for him.

During wars, soldiers often get lice. Maybe this is because they live in crowded barracks where it's easy for a louse to fall off one soldier and crawl onto the soldier sleeping next to him. Soldiers call lice "cooties" or "mechanical dandruff."

During World War I, a doctor counted 10,428 lice and 10,253 eggs on just one soldier's shirt!

Squeeze! There's always room for one more.

Lice have stuck around people for so long because they are parasites, and that means they need us. Parasites are animals that don't go out and get their own food. They live on another animal and eat *it* instead.

The other animal is called the host. When lice live on you, you are the host and they eat—you!

Lice don't take bites out of their host. They suck its blood. In a louse's mouth, there are three pointy tubes called stylets. Just like you poke a straw into a juice box and suck out the juice, a louse pokes its stylets into its host and sucks out a little bit of blood.

Lice can live in your hair, on your body, or in the seams of your clothes. Head lice are the kind that live in your hair. They use their tiny claws to hold on to the hairs on your head. They hold on so tightly that just brushing your hair or washing it with regular shampoo won't get rid of them.

Like many other insects, lice have learned that it's best to blend in. Lice can be different colors, depending on the color of their host.

Lice in Africa are dark because most people in Africa have dark skin. Lice in Europe are light. Lice in Japan are tan. And lice in America are—you guessed it!—all different colors from light to dark.

Lice are smaller than grains of rice. They are so small that their stylets don't hurt when they make holes in your skin.

However, lice have very bad manners. After they drink, they spit in the holes that they made. The spit keeps your blood from thickening and making a scab.

The spit also makes you itch. The more you itch, the more you scratch. If you scratch hard enough, you will bleed more, and the louse will have another snack without doing any work at all.

Fortunately, lice live for only about a month. But they have lots of babies. A mother louse can lay 75 to 100 eggs in her lifetime. She lays the eggs on a strand of hair close to your scalp where it's nice and warm.

Rock-a-bye, baby.

The eggs are small—as small as the head of a pin—and white. They are called nits. The word "nit-picking" means looking so closely that you always find something wrong. Nits are so tiny that you have to look very closely to find them, and when you've found one, look for more.

The baby louse stays in its egg for five to eight days. Then it pokes its head out through a tiny trapdoor at one end. It sees a jungle of hair—and lunch below it. To get out, the baby louse takes a deep breath, then another, and another, until it puffs up so big that it pops right out of its egg.

So how do you get rid of lice? First of all, try not to get them. Lice can't fly, and they can't jump. Their little claw feet can't crawl far or fast. As long as their host is feeding them, they don't want to travel.

Don't provide them with transportation. Don't borrow anything that's been on someone else's head. Don't trade combs, brushes, hats, barrettes, headbands, or scarves. A louse might be along for the ride.

Some people think you get lice because you're dirty. But you can wash your hair every day and still get lice—if you borrow your best friend's comb and she has lice. You can wash your hair only once a week and never get lice—as long as you don't borrow anyone's comb or brush, don't let anyone borrow yours, and don't trade hats or headwear. Being clean isn't what counts; what counts is being careful.

If you do get lice—

Have your parents write a note to your teacher and the school nurse.

Be extra careful not to share brushes, combs, hats, or headbands with your friends or family.

Your doctor or pharmacist will give you a special shampoo. Be sure to follow the instructions exactly.

Ask an adult to pick out the nits for you. It may take a long time, so be patient.

Soak all your combs, brushes, barrettes, and headbands for ten minutes in hot, soapy water.

Wash everything—all your sheets, pillowcases, hats, towels, stuffed animals, coats—in hot water and dry them in the dryer.

Anything that can't be washed should be sealed in a plastic bag for 30 days.

27

Long ago, lice were a serious problem. People didn't know what caused lice. They didn't know how to get rid of them. Some people even liked having lice because they thought lice were good for them.

Today, we know more about lice. We have shampoos and medicines that prevent serious lice epidemics. Doctors, nurses, and teachers know how to spot lice early. If we all work together, maybe someday lice will no longer be a problem at all.

PReVeNtiOn and TreAtMent

Headlice are the second most common communicable childhood disease, following colds. But unlike colds, lice cause embarrassment for children and their families. Many people still believe that only people with poor hygiene habits get lice. This is not true. Anyone can get lice.

The best way to prevent lice is not to borrow hats, brushes, combs, headbands, or barrettes—anything that has touched someone else's head. You may also want to consider the following as possible sources of lice: sleeping bags and bedding at slumber parties; seats in movie theaters, cars, and airplanes; dress-up clothes; stuffed animals; and headphones. Children may be reluctant to say "no" when someone asks to borrow a comb or brush from them; counsel them in ways to say it politely but firmly.

Headlice are treated with special shampoos that you can obtain from your doctor or pharmacist. These products are serious medicine. Take them seriously. Long-term use can harm children. In order to avoid using them too often, you must remove *all* lice and nits from the child's head after shampooing with the lice shampoo. Use a fine-toothed comb on one small section of hair at a time. Then look at each hair for nits, usually at the root but sometimes along the hair shaft. All bedding and clothing should be washed, and all carpets and upholstery vacuumed. It's a good idea to check every member of the family, too.

OtHer BooKs for YoU and YoUr ParEntS

MORE BOOKS FOR YOU

Caffey, Donna. *Yikes—Lice!* Whitman, a division of Western Publishing Co., New York: 1998.

Blassingame, Wyatt. *The Little Killers.* G.P. Putnam's Sons, New York: 1975.

Gilson, Jamie. *Itchy Richard.* Clarion Books, New York: 1991.

Goldstein, Philip and Margaret. *How Parasites Live.* Holiday House, New York: 1976.

BOOKS FOR YOUR PARENTS OR TEACHERS

Copeland, Lennie. *The Lice-Buster Book.* Authentic Pictures, Mill Valley, CA: 1995.

Moore, Wayne S. *Controlling Household Pests.* Ortho Books, San Ramon, CA: 1988.

Zinsser, Hans. *Rats, Lice and History.* Black Dog and Levanthal Publishers, New York: 1934.